I0559496

Cross Stitch Cats

5 Counted Cross Stitch Patterns

by Kay Goodnight

ISBN 979-8-8040497-2-1

About the Author

Kay Goodnight enjoys crafts of all kinds – cross stitch, crochet, jewelry making, and water color painting among others. She has also published several books for children including PETDEMONIUM, MISTWIZZLED, SIDEWAYS WISHES and THE ADVENTURES OF PB AND JAY, a series for early readers.

Cross stitch is one of the easiest forms of needle work to learn. It is comprised of X-shaped stitches done side by side in a variety of colors to form words, patterns, and/or pictures.

Some cross stitch projects are sold as kits, but you can easily purchase fabric, thread and other supplies for your own project.

Reading Cross Stitch Charts/Patterns

A cross stitch chart tells you where to stitch and what colors to use for a project. Each square on the chart represents one cross stitch on your fabric.

The symbols within each square tell you which color of floss to use. A chart legend is included that translates these symbols into a specific floss color. Some charts, usually black and white, use symbols only. Others, color charts, use color and symbols to detail the design.

Arrows on the top and side of the chart indicate the center of your project.

To help you keep your place and count accurately, every tenth line in a chart is a little darker, both horizontally and vertically.

For these lessons, we'll use this simple **Bumblebee** chart. It utilizes only two colors, black and medium yellow, with backstitching in black.

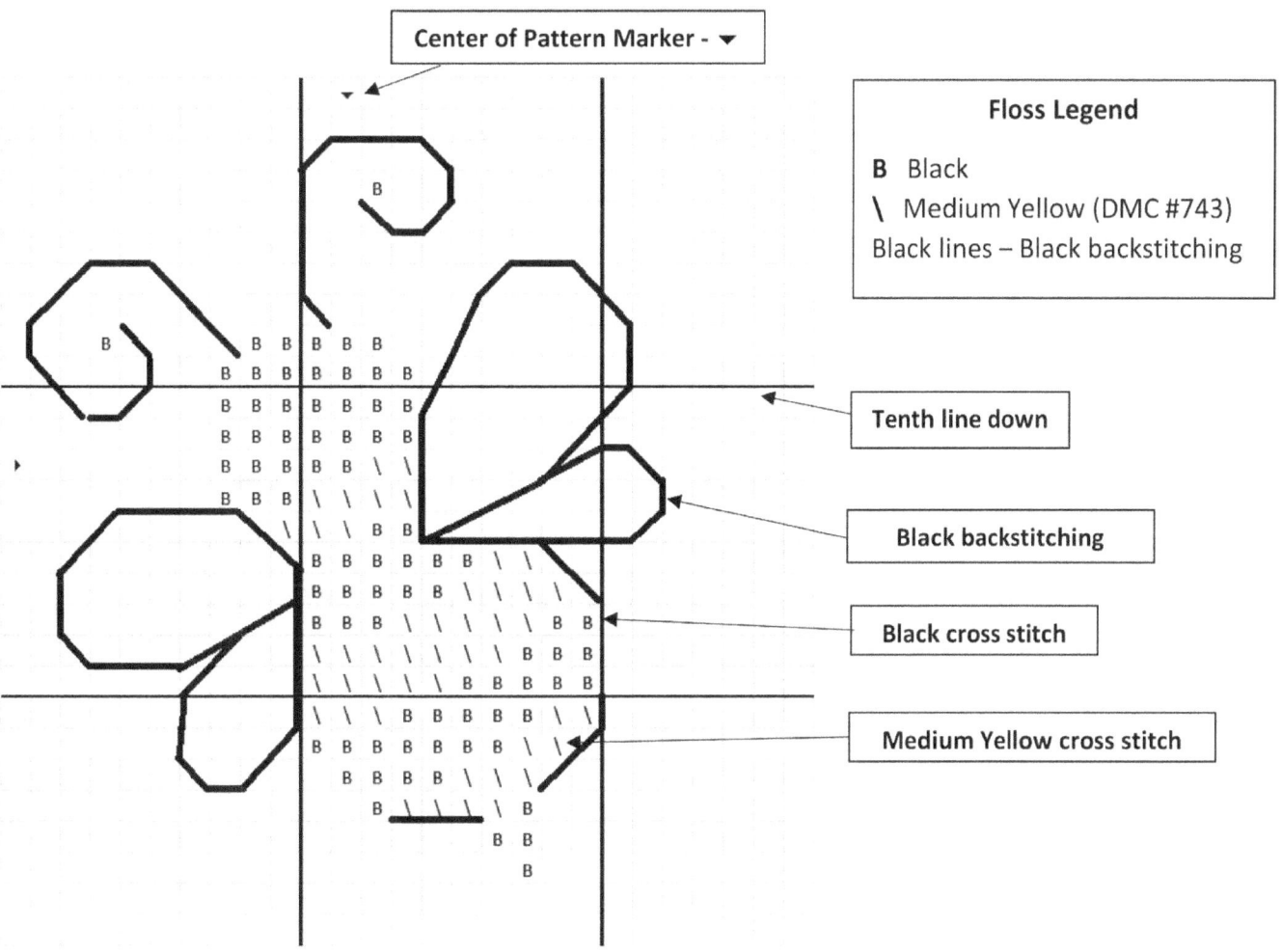

Basic Supplies

Whether you choose to use a kit or buy all your own supplies, each project requires the same basic supplies.

Embroidery Hoop (optional)

- A 4" hoop works well for the designs in this book. However, hoops come in a large variety of sizes to fit your needs.

Embroidery Thread (Floss)

- In this book, there are 8 to 12 colors per pattern.

- The DMC floss colors and numbers are listed with each pattern.

- It's wise to buy all your floss for a project at the start. Thread comes in dye lots that may vary slightly between batches.

Scissors

Cross Stitch Needle

- These have a larger loop for threading the floss and duller tip than other needles since the fabric used already has holes.

Fabric

- Using Aida 14 count fabric will result in the finished size indicated on each of the patterns in this book. However, these patterns can be used with larger or smaller count fabrics as well as with plastic cross stitch canvas.

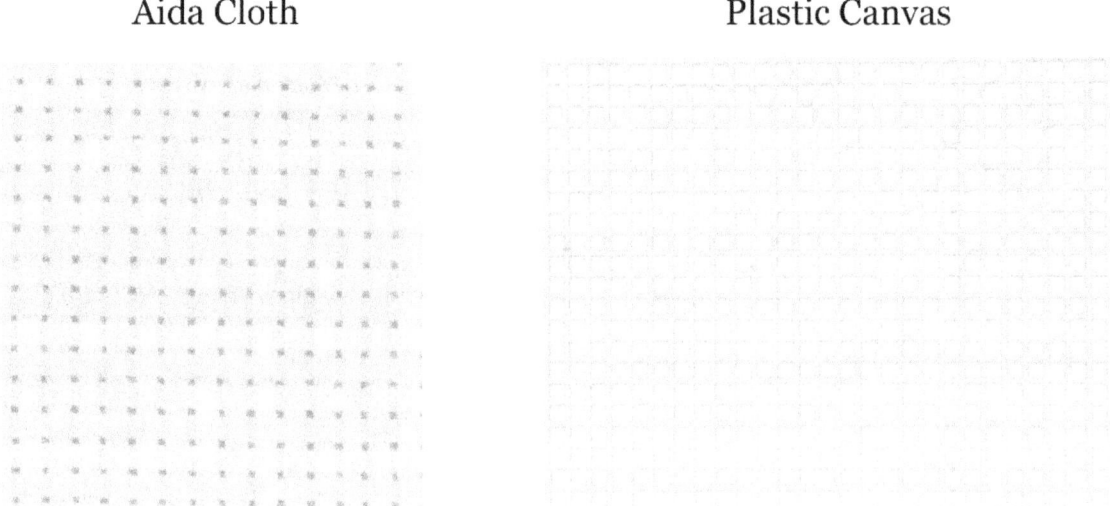

Aida Cloth   Plastic Canvas

Keeping Your Place

Using some kind of straight edge will help you keep your place on the chart. Place one straight edge horizontally on your chart and, if desired, a second one vertically.

- Cross Stitch Line Keepers (magnetically attach to your chart)

- Sticky Notes (my personal favorite)

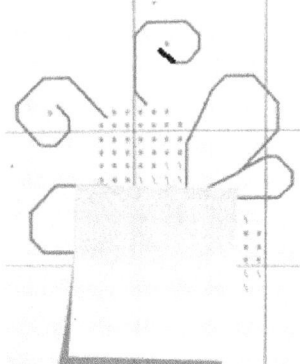

- Rulers

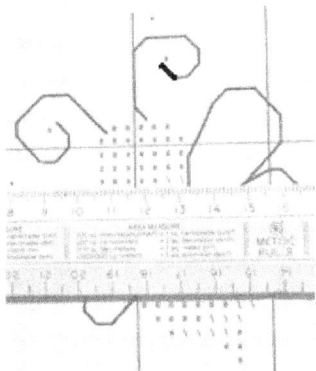

- Index Cards

- Painter's Tape (peels off easily for repositioning)

Getting Started

Preparing Your Fabric

a. Cut fabric to the needed size plus 2 or 3 inches on each side. For example, the **Bumblebee** pattern is 1 ½" by 1 ¾". You'll need to add a minimum of 4 inches to the width (2" for the left side plus 2" for the right side) and 4 inches to the height (2" to the top plus 2" to the bottom).

> The **Bumblebee's** finished size on 14 count Aida is 1 ½" by 1 ¾"
> Add 4 inches to the width: 4 + 1 ½ = 5 ½ inches
> Add 4 inches to the height: 4 + 1 ¾ = 5 ¾ inches
> So cut your fabric 5 ½" by 5 ¾" for our **Bumblebee** project.

This will:

1. Allow the fabric to be secured comfortably in an embroidery hoop

2. Give flexibility for finishing (framing, sewing borders, etc.)

3. Provide extra fabric in case of fraying (see below)

b. Since Aida fabric is such a loose weave, it tends to fray. To prevent this, you can:

   a. Cut the fabric with pinking shears, or

   b. Sew the edges with a zig-zag stitch, or

   c. Tape the edges with masking tape.

Pinking Shears	Zig-Zag Stitch	Tape

c. To ensure that your finished design is centered on the fabric, find the center of the cloth.

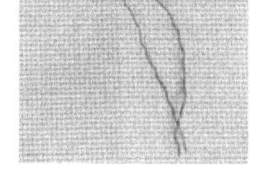

   a. Fold it once horizontally and gently crease.

   b. Fold it once vertically and gently crease.

   c. Sew the intersection with a piece of thread to mark the spot.

   NOTE: This thread will be removed once you've begun your project.

d. If desired, gently secure your fabric into an embroidery hoop, tight enough to hold it but not so tight that it stretches the fabric (see the next page).

Using a Hoop

Using a hoop is not required. It's a matter of personal preference. Beginning cross stitch crafters may find it easier to use a hoop.

a. Loosen the screw on the hoop and separate the two round parts.

b. Place the round part without the screw flat on a table.

c. Center the fabric over the hoop.

d. Place the other round part with the screw over the fabric and gently press down so the fabric is seated between the two hoops.

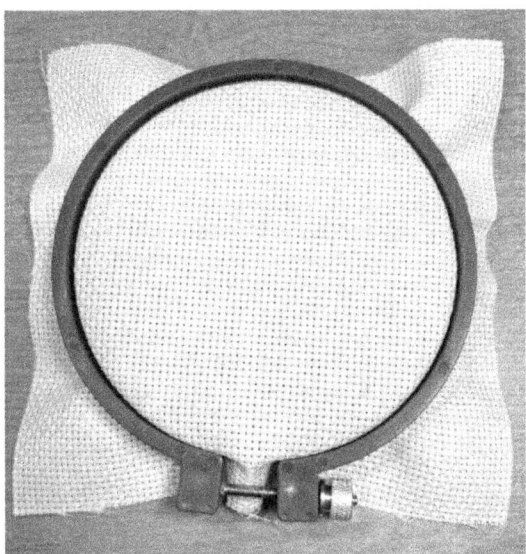

e. Pull the fabric taut as you gradually tighten the screw, being careful not to distort the weave of the fabric.

Preparing Your Floss

Embroidery floss is comprised of six strands twisted together. You will usually be working with two strands at a time.

6 Strands

    a. Cut a length of floss from the skein.

    b. Gently pull the needed number of strands from the length of floss you just cut, taking care not to tangle the thread as it unwinds.

Threading Your Floss

The number of floss strands you insert through your needle depends on how you plan to anchor it so that it doesn't pull through as you stitch. Here are three ways to anchor your floss.

1) The **knot method** is exactly what it sounds like. A knot will anchor your thread. Use this method for small projects you have a hard time starting and for when the look of the back doesn't matter.

    a. Cut approximately an 18 inch (46 cm) piece of floss and pull out two strands.

    b. Thread both strands through the needle.

    c. Tie a knot at one end of the pair of strands.

    d. Start stitching.

       NOTE: Generally, you'll want to avoid using knots in your cross stitching because it could leave lumps in your final project.

2) With the **bury method**, you bury the thread on the back under the first few stitches.

    a. Cut approximately an 18 inch (46 cm) piece of floss and pull out two strands.

    b. Thread both strands through the needle.

    c. Start stitching making sure to catch your thread on the back for the next three or four stitches.

    d. Trim.

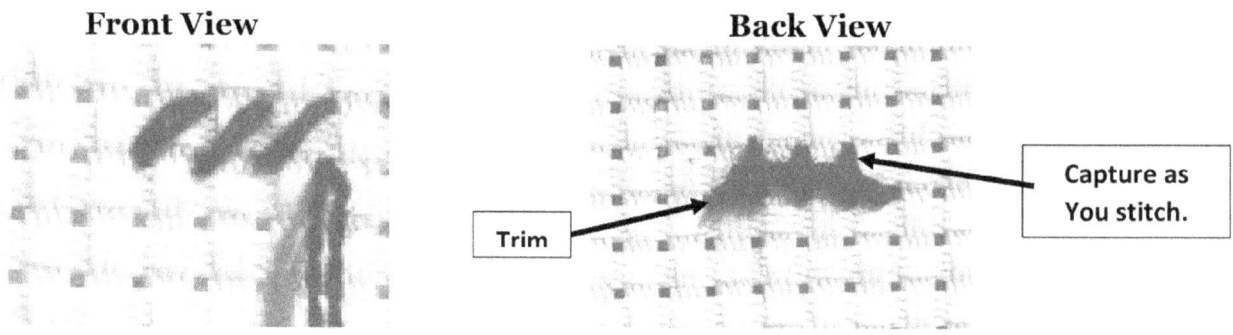

Front View   **Back View**

Trim

Capture as You stitch.

3) The **loop method** anchors your thread in a single stitch and works really well for small projects.

   a. Cut approximately a 36 inch (60 cm) piece of floss and pull out ONE strand.

   b. Thread BOTH ends of the single strand of thread through your needle so there is a loop at the bottom.

   c. Start your stitch (up once, down once).

   d. A loop will form on the back. Put your needle through the loop and pull to tighten the anchor.

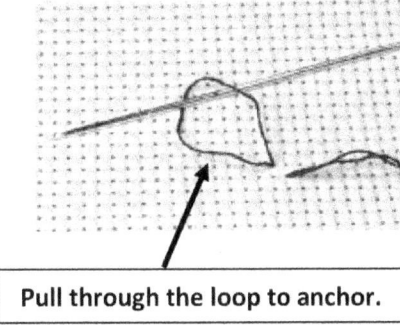

Pull through the loop to anchor.

Where to Begin

It is a good idea to start in the center of your project to ensure it is also centered on the cloth, but this may depend on the project and its size.

You don't have to start in the exact center of your design. It may be easiest to find a large block of one color near the center to give a reference point from which to orient the rest of your work.

Let's take another look at our **Bumblebee** pattern. We want to start stitching in the center of the design. As previously shown, the center is indicated by small arrows at the sides of the pattern (▾). If we follow the arrow at the top down and the one at the left across, we see that the color at the center of the design is **B** for **black floss**.

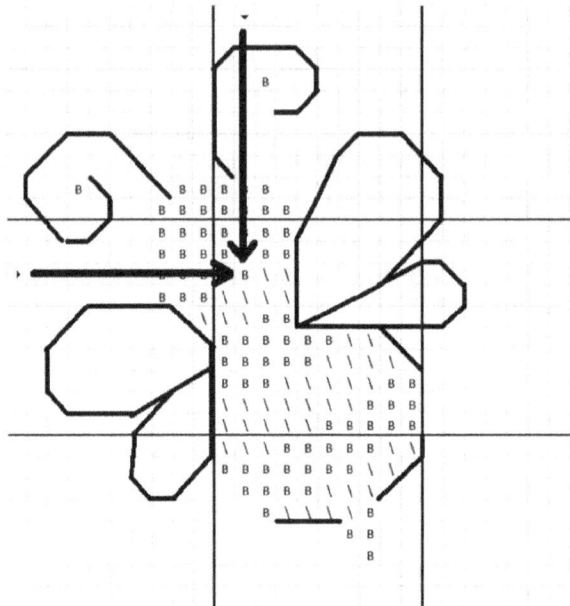

The center color's row starts four stiches to the left of center. But the entire BLOCK of color B starts four stitches left and one row down.

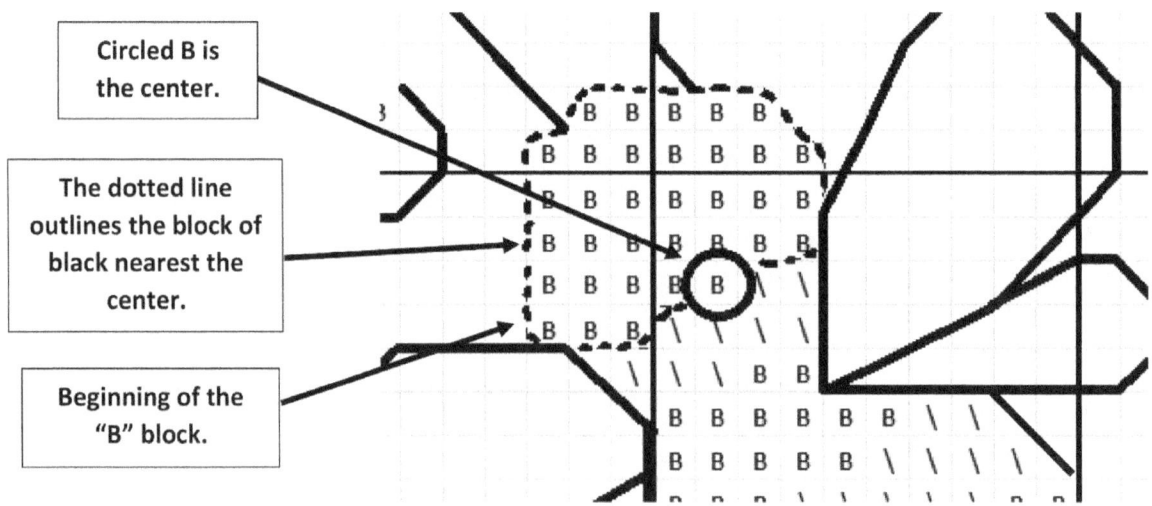

Circled B is the center.

The dotted line outlines the block of black nearest the center.

Beginning of the "B" block.

10

We'll be working from left to right and bottom to top. So we'll start our first stitch in the bottom left hole five columns to the left of our center thread and one row down.

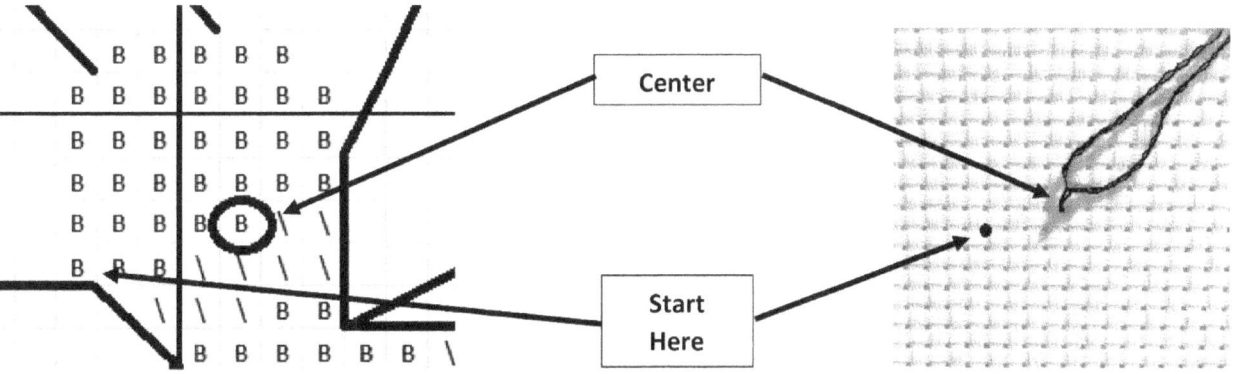

NOTE: Always double check and recount to make sure you are starting in the right place.

Your First Stitches

a. Starting from the back, go up through the bottom left hole, leaving about a one inch tail on your thread (if you're going to use the "capture method" to anchor your thread). Then stitch down through the top right hole that's diagonal from the first one (/). Keep a nice easy tension on your stitches. Pulling them too tight will warp the fabric. Leaving them too loose will cause gaps in your project. The stitches should lie flat against the fabric without pulling against it.

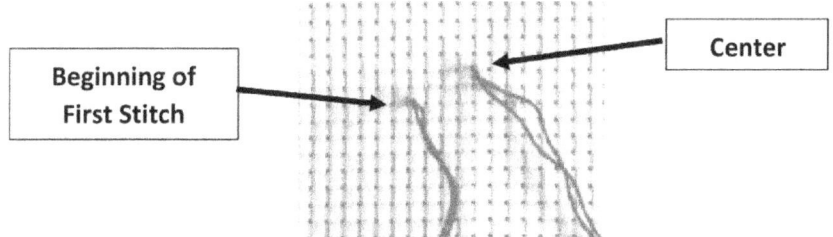

b. The black has 3 stiches on that row. So repeat two more times – up through the bottom left hole and down through the top right hole, capturing the tail of your thread at the back as you stitch.

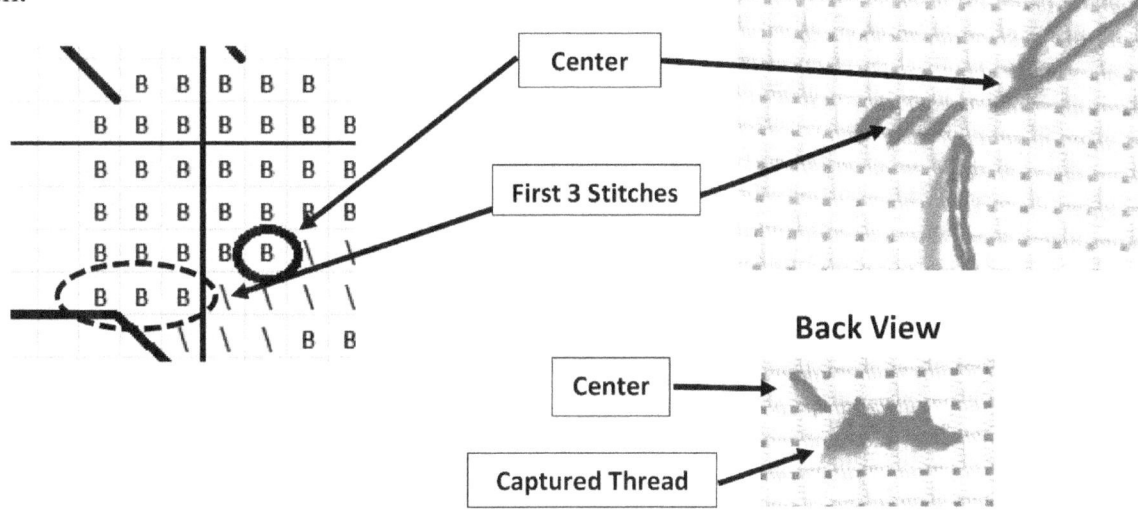

c. To complete the cross on these stitches, now go up through the bottom right hole and down through the top left.

d. Since you no longer need it, remove the middle thread.

IMPORTANT: For the neatest look on your finished product, keep the direction of the bottom stitches and the direction of your top stitches the same throughout the project. So if you start by stitching bottom left to top right (/), then cross it with a stitch that goes bottom right to top left (\ ). Now maintain that pattern for your stitch directions throughout the piece.

Rows 2 through 6

The next row of black is above the three stitches you just completed. But to continue the bottom left/top right pattern, you'd have to go down the same stitch you just came up. So instead:

a. Go to the next row up.

b. Stitch from the top right (1) down to the bottom left (2) so your bottom stitch of the X will be a /.

c. For the next stitch, you can resume the bottom left (3) / top right (4) pattern.

d. Continue for three more stitches as shown on the pattern.

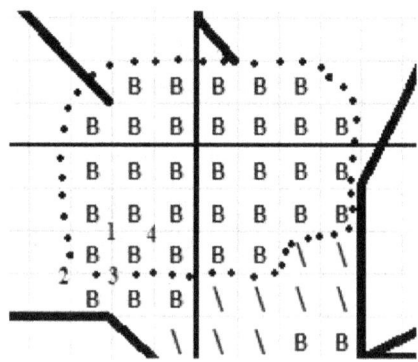

e. Go up through the bottom right and down through the top left to complete the crosses.

f. Continue for the rest of the rows in the block.

Ending a Color/Strand

To end a color and/or start a new strand:

a. Turn your work over to the back.

b. Thread your floss beneath several stitches on the back. If you wish, thread your floss through a second row as well for additional security.

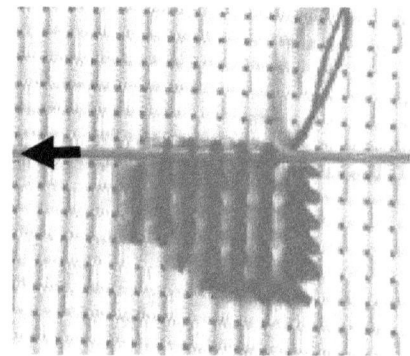

c. Trim.

Traveling

Traveling in cross stitching is bringing a color from one section to the next section across blank spaces or spaces filled with other colors.

It is best to travel no more than 2 or 3 stitches across blank fabric.

Making long jumps across the back of your fabric, especially with dark threads, will cause a shadow on your project that will show through from the front. So when moving more than 2 or 3 stitches to a new area you should either:

- End your thread and begin again in the new section.

    OR

- Turn your work over and thread the floss through the backs of existing stitches. This will hide them until you come out just above where you wish to begin your new section.

For example, we started with black on the **Bumblebee** pattern. If we travel with the black thread from one block of black to the next, it will show through (cast a shadow) onto the front of your finished piece.

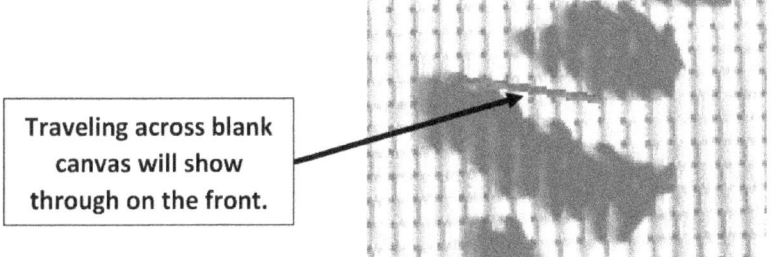

Traveling across blank canvas will show through on the front.

A better plan would be to tie off your strand at the end of each block before starting a new one.

Back View

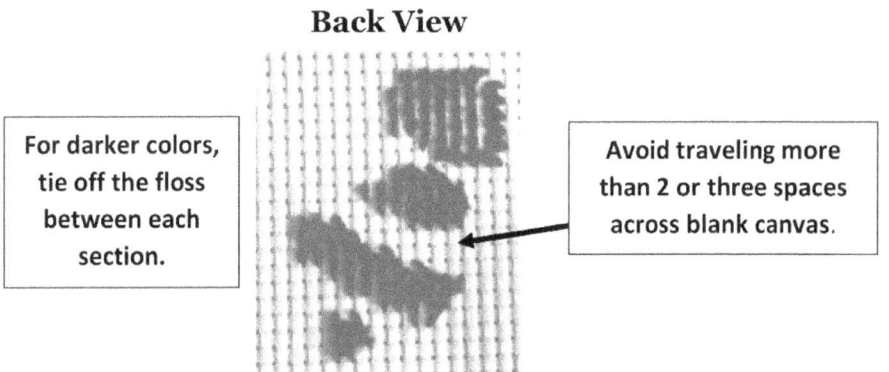

For darker colors, tie off the floss between each section.

Avoid traveling more than 2 or three spaces across blank canvas.

However, once you begin to fill in with the yellow, you could "travel" across the black to the next section and the lighter yellow color will be hidden by the existing darker black and won't show through.

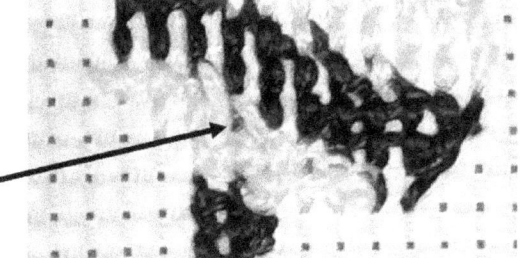

Traveled a couple of stitches over black to begin the next row.

Back Stitching (Straight Stitching)

Back stitching allows you to outline or add details to your project (i.e. cat's whiskers, outline of lighter areas, flower steams). It can also be used to personalize a pattern (i.e. stitcher's name, date completed, a message to the person its being gifted to).

Back stitching is usually done in a darker color with a single strand of thread (unless otherwise indicated on a pattern).

It can be every stitch, skip stitches, or go diagonally.

It is usually shown by a thin black line across a pattern. In this book, a second chart is included showing the back stitching for each pattern so the back stitching 'lines' don't cover up any of the color codes.

Anchor your back stitch thread under one of your cross stitched rows.

Up once and down once makes a single back stitch. Then go 'back' to avoid going up the same stitch you just came down.

Here's a diagram of how to back stitch the left antenna of our **Bumblebee**.

a) Anchor your single thread under a row of black cross stitches or use the loop method.

b) Stitch 1: Go up at 2 and down at 1.

c) Stitch 2: Go up at 3 and down at 2.

d) Stitch 3: Go up at 4 and down at 3.

e) Stitch 4: Go up at 5 and down at 4.

f) Continue until you reach the center.

g) Finish with a single cross stitch in the middle.

h) Run the thread back through several stitches to tie it off.

i) Trim your thread.

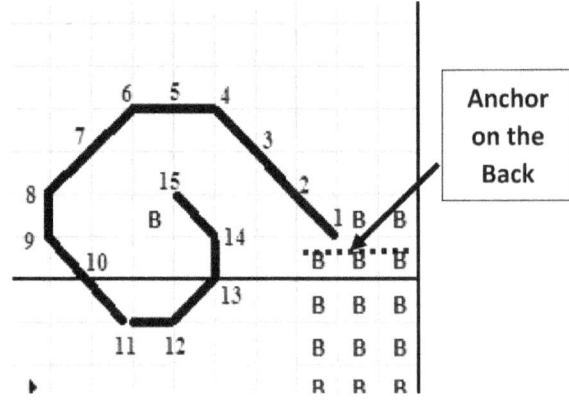

Front

Back

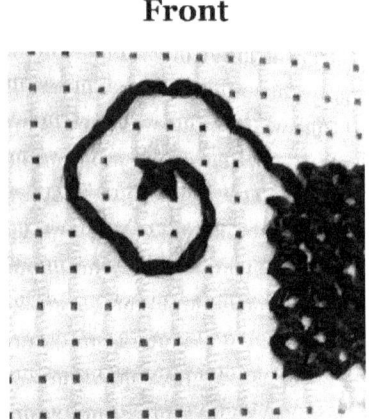

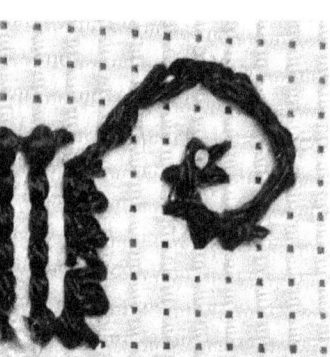

Working with Multiple Colors

Some people like to do all of one color before changing to the next.

Others may prefer to finish an area of their project before moving on. Do whichever works best for you and the current project you're working on.

If you are working an area with multiple colors, consider using multiple needles as well. That way you can have all the colors you need readily available without having to stop and start in order to rethread a needle.

Planning Ahead

Depending on where one row of stitches of the same color ends and the next row begins, you may not always be able to follow the pattern of bottom left/top right and reverse because you'd have to go down the same hole you just came up (see Page 12 - **Rows 2 through 6**).

Plan ahead as you near the end of each row.

You also want to avoid skipping across several stitches of blank canvas (see Page 13 – **Traveling**) to get to the next stitch of the same color.

Other Tips

Typically, it is easier to work from left to right and top to bottom.

As you work, the thread tends to twist. When you notice this, let your needle hang freely for a moment so it can unwind.

Buy all your floss for one project at one time. The same color from different dye lots may vary slightly.

Avoid eating and drinking while cross-stitching and ALWAYS work with clean hands.

Most importantly, ***HAVE A BEE-UTIFUL TIME!***

Cat Napping Details

General Information

Fabric count: 14 count Aida

Stitches: 50 by 54

Total skeins: 9

Finished size: 3.5" by 3.8"

Total Stitches: 1,714

Floss type: DMC

DMC Embroidery Floss Color Code

↗	D02	Tin	Stitches: 305 – Skeins: 1
☽	D310	Black	Stitches: 370 – Skeins: 1
O	D413	Pewter Gray DK	Stitches: 5 – Skeins: 1
↶	D601	Cranberry DK	Stitches: 189 – Skeins: 1
◢	D722	Orange Spice LT	Stitches: 27 – Skeins: 1
↕	D796	Royal Blue DK	Stitches: 142 – Skeins: 1
▲	D799	Delft Blue MD	Stitches: 49 – Skeins: 1
+	D800	Pale Delft Blue	Stitches: 235 – Skeins: 1
↑	DBLANC	White	Stitches: 111 – Skeins: 1

Back Stitching (page 18)

Eyes and Nose: D310 Black

Cat Napping (**Without** Backstitching)

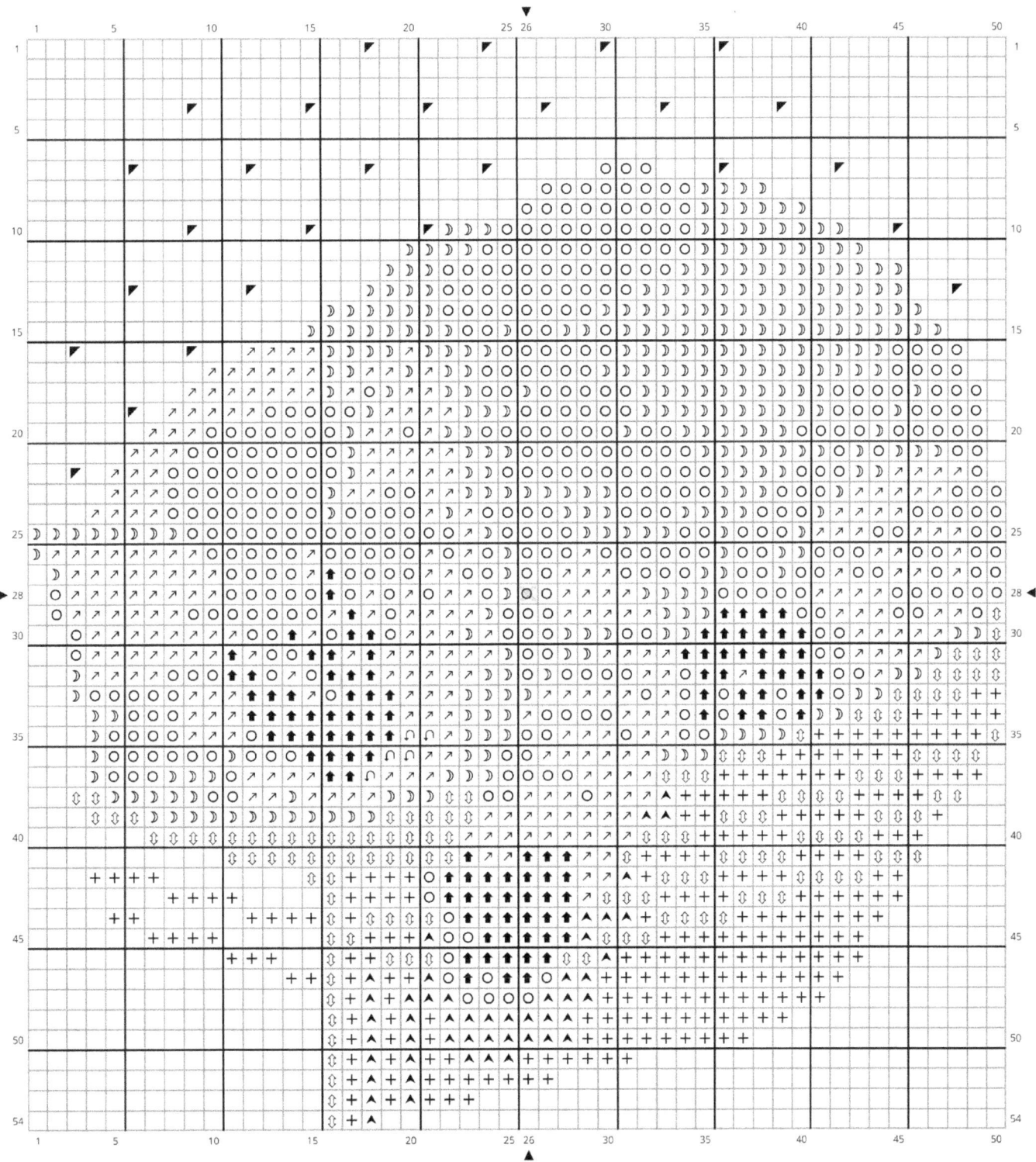

Cat Napping (**WITH** Backstitching)

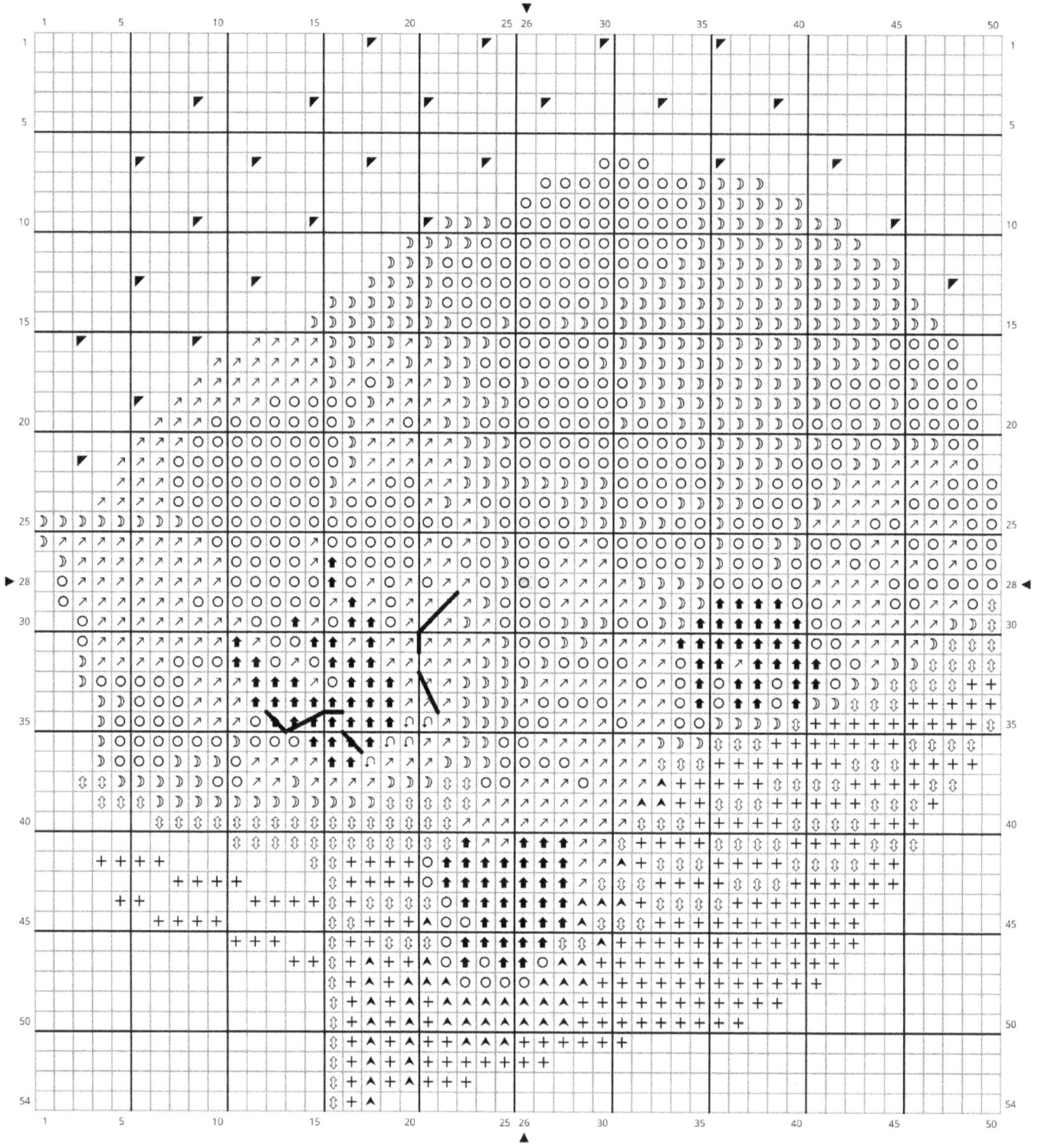

Eyes and Nose: Black

A Bit of a Yarn Details

General Information

Fabric count: 14 count Aida

Stitches: 54 by 57

Total skeins: 12

Finished size: 3.8" by 4"

Total Stitches: 1,330

Floss type: DMC

DMC Embroidery Floss Color Code

⇩	D310	Black	Stitches: 2 – Skeins: 1
✳	D601	Cranberry DK	Stitches: 6 – Skeins: 1
⬅	D800	Pale Delft Blue	Stitches: 56 – Skeins: 1
↕	D838	Beige Brown VY DK	Stitches: 257 – Skeins: 1
⬆	D840	Beige Brown MD	Stitches: 160 – Skeins: 1
➡	D841	Beige Brown LT	Stitches: 327 – Skeins: 1
◀	D842	Beige Brown VY LT	Stitches: 180 – Skeins: 1
↖	D937	Avocado Green MD	Stitches: 18 – Skeins: 1
◆	D967	Apricot VY LT	Stitches: 25 – Skeins: 1
↑	D3340	Apricot MD	Stitches: 167 – Skeins: 1
→	D3341	Apricot	Stitches: 74 – Skeins: 1
⇇	DBLANC	White	Stitches: 58 – Skeins: 1

Back Stitching (page 21)

Mouth, Paws, and Yarn Shadowing: D838 Beige Brown Very Dark

Floor Tiles: D841 Beige Brown LT

Eye Highlights: White

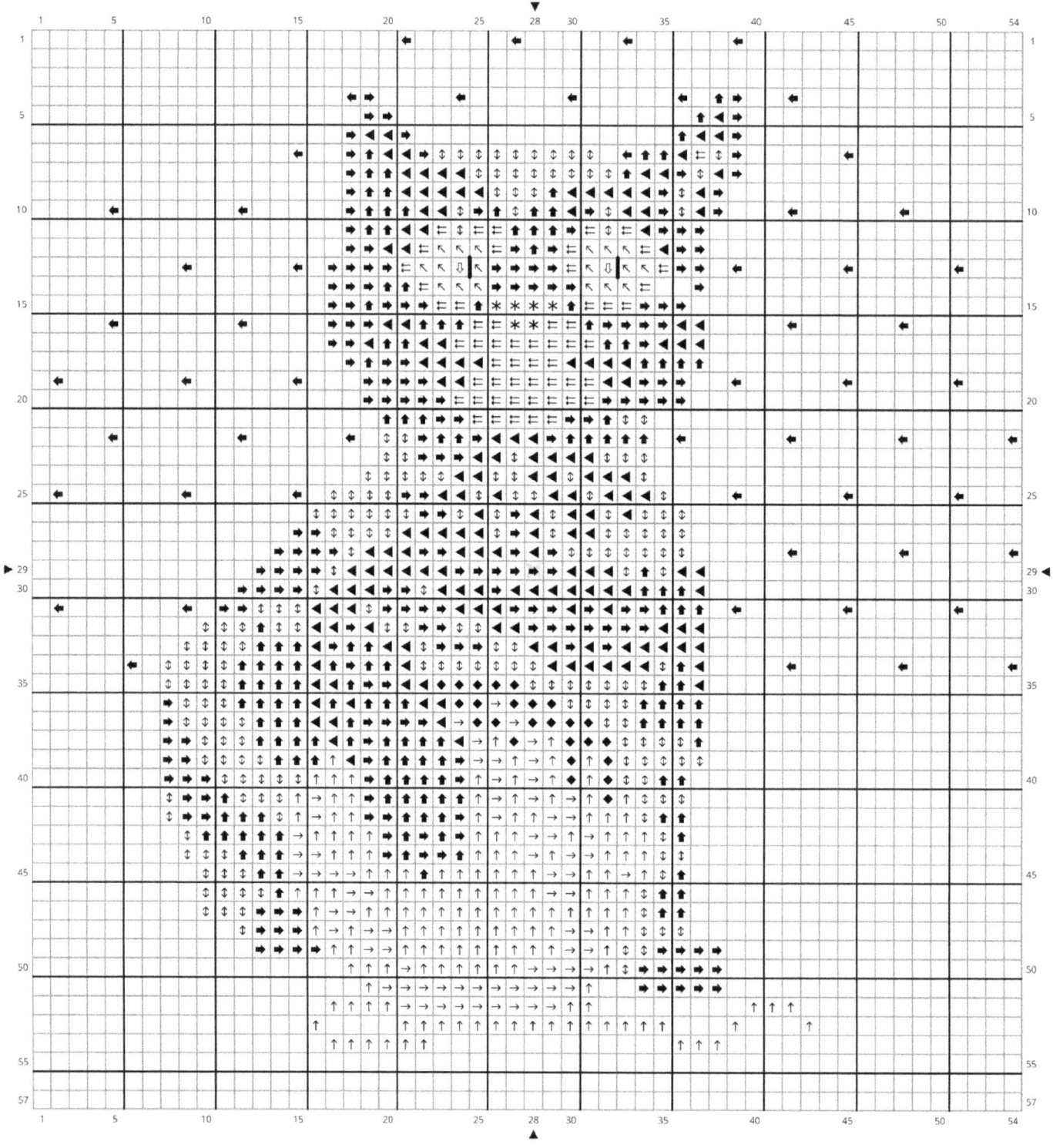

A Bit of a Yarn (**WITH** Backstitching)

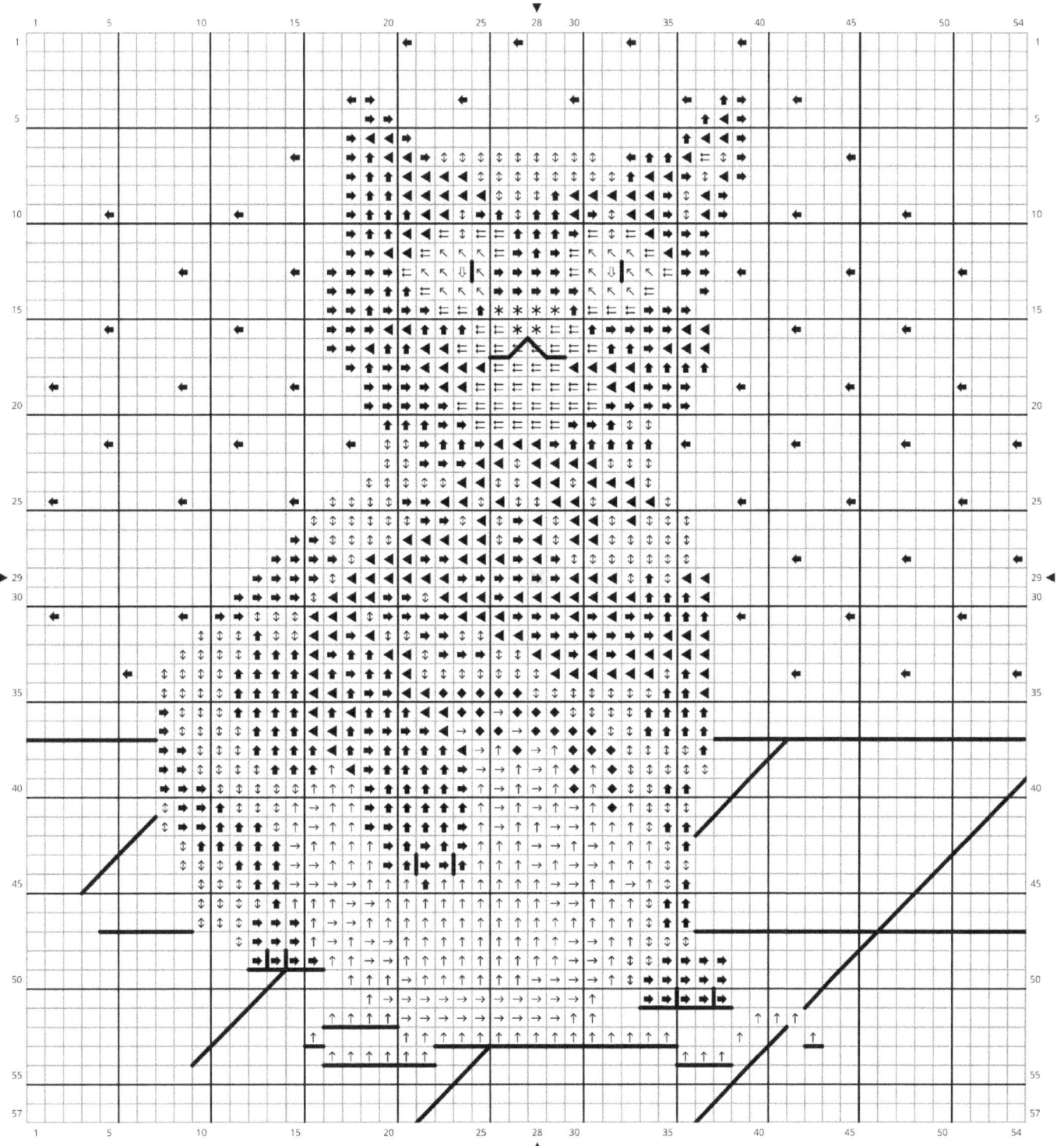

Peeping Thomas

General Information

Fabric count: 14 count Aida

Stitches: 51 by 46

Total skeins: 11

Finished size: 3.6" by 3.2"

Total Stitches: 1,422

Floss type: DMC

DMC Embroidery Floss Color Code

⊙	D02	Tin	Stitches: 147 – Skeins: 1
←	D310	Black	Stitches: 8 – Skeins: 1
↖	D677	Old Gold VY LT	Stitches: 95 – Skeins: 1
↯	D726	Topaz LT	Stitches: 225– Skeins: 1
➡	D797	Royal Blue	Stitches: 102 – Skeins: 1
^	D800	Pale Delft Blue	Stitches: 169 – Skeins: 1
↗	D3812	Sea Green VY DK	Stitches: 98 – Skeins: 1
▶	D3831	Raspberry DK	Stitches: 128 – Skeins: 1
↓	D3833	Raspberry LT	Stitches: 65 – Skeins: 1
+	DBLANC	White	Stitches: 242 – Skeins: 1

Backstitching: D317 Pewter Gray   Stitches: 143 – Skeins: 1

Back Stitching (page 24)

Mouth and Windowsill: D317 Dark Pewter Gray

Windowpane Shimmer: D800 Pale Delft Blue

Peeping Thomas (Without Backstitching)

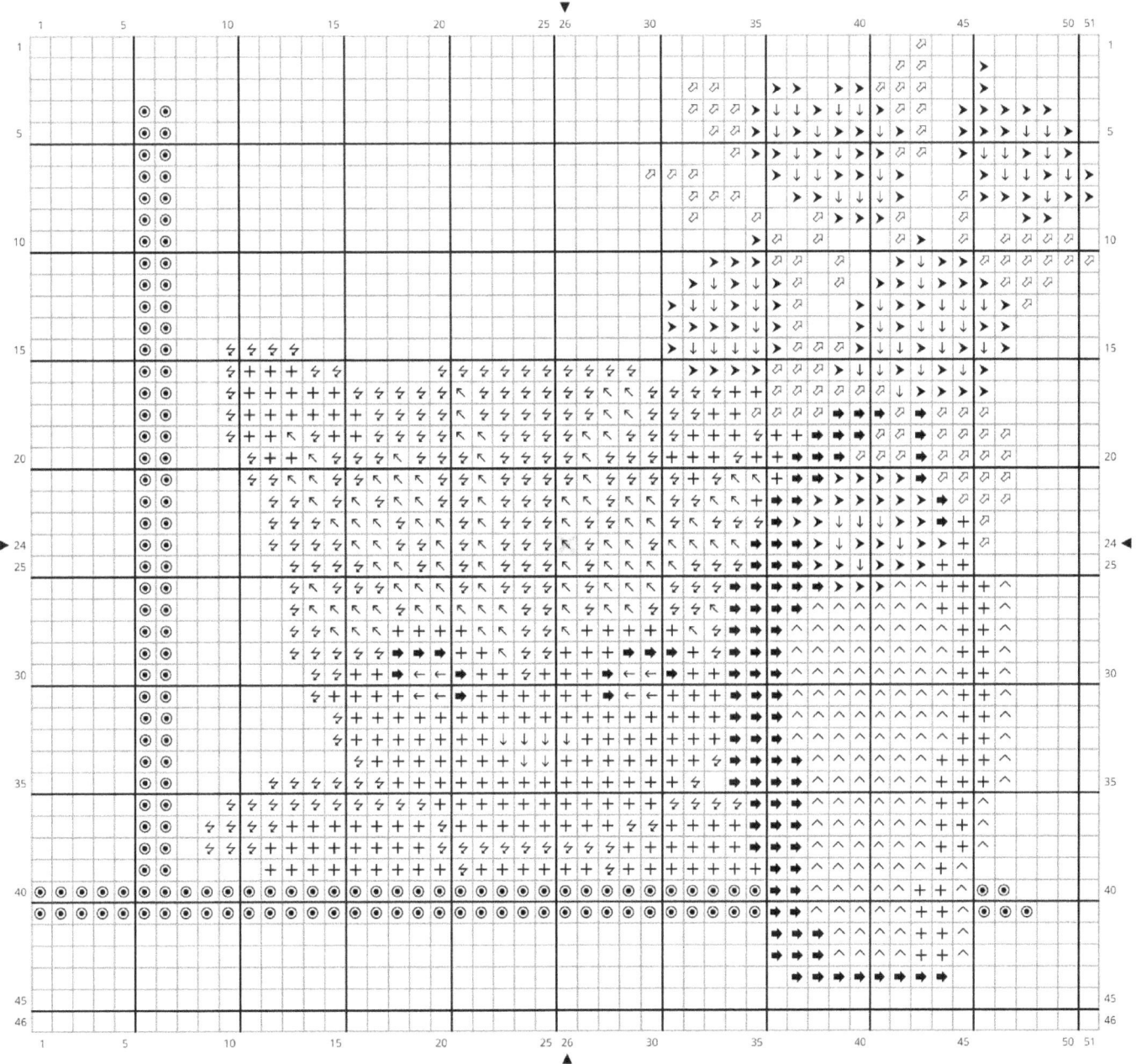

Peeping Thomas (**WITH** Backstitching)

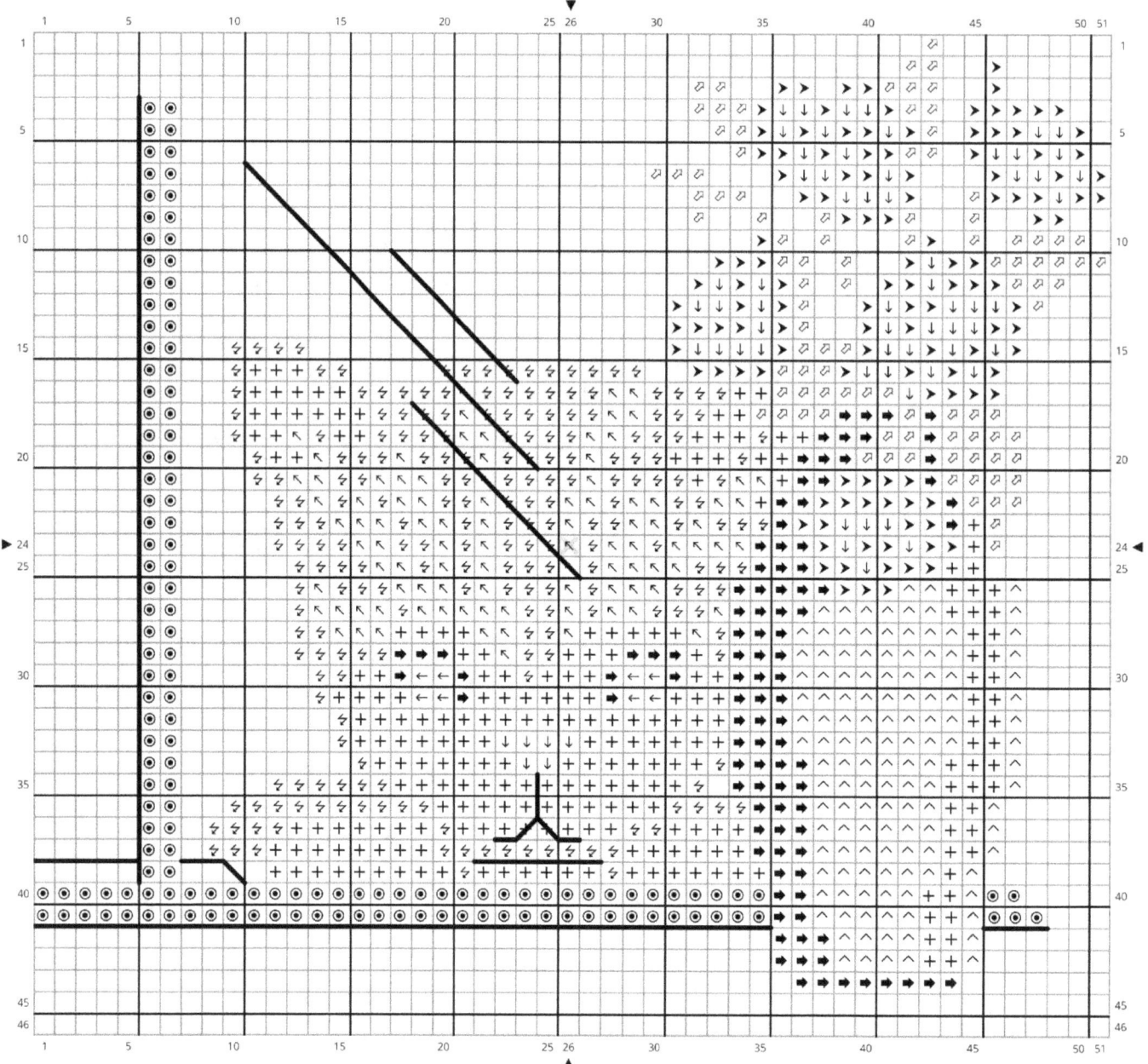

On The Hunt

General Information

Fabric count: 14 count Aida

Stitches: 60 by 57

Total skeins: 8

Finished size: 4.2" by 4"

Total Stitches: 1,577

Floss type: DMC

DMC Embroidery Floss Color Code

⇧	D01	White Tin	Stitches: 192 – Skeins: 1
⇨	D310	Black	Stitches: 139 – Skeins: 1
⇦	D413	Pewter Gray DK	Stitches: 660 – Skeins: 1
◀	D505	Jade Green	Stitches: 49 – Skeins: 1
⇇	D3341	Apricot	Stitches: 52 – Skeins: 1
↺	D3698	Mauve LT	Stitches: 4 – Skeins: 1
◖	D3761	Sky Blue LT	Stitches: 243 – Skeins: 1

Backstitching: D996   Electric Blue MD   Stitches: 238 – Skeins: 1

Back Stitching (page 27)

Paws and Mouth: D310 Black

Fishbowl: D996 Electric Blue MD

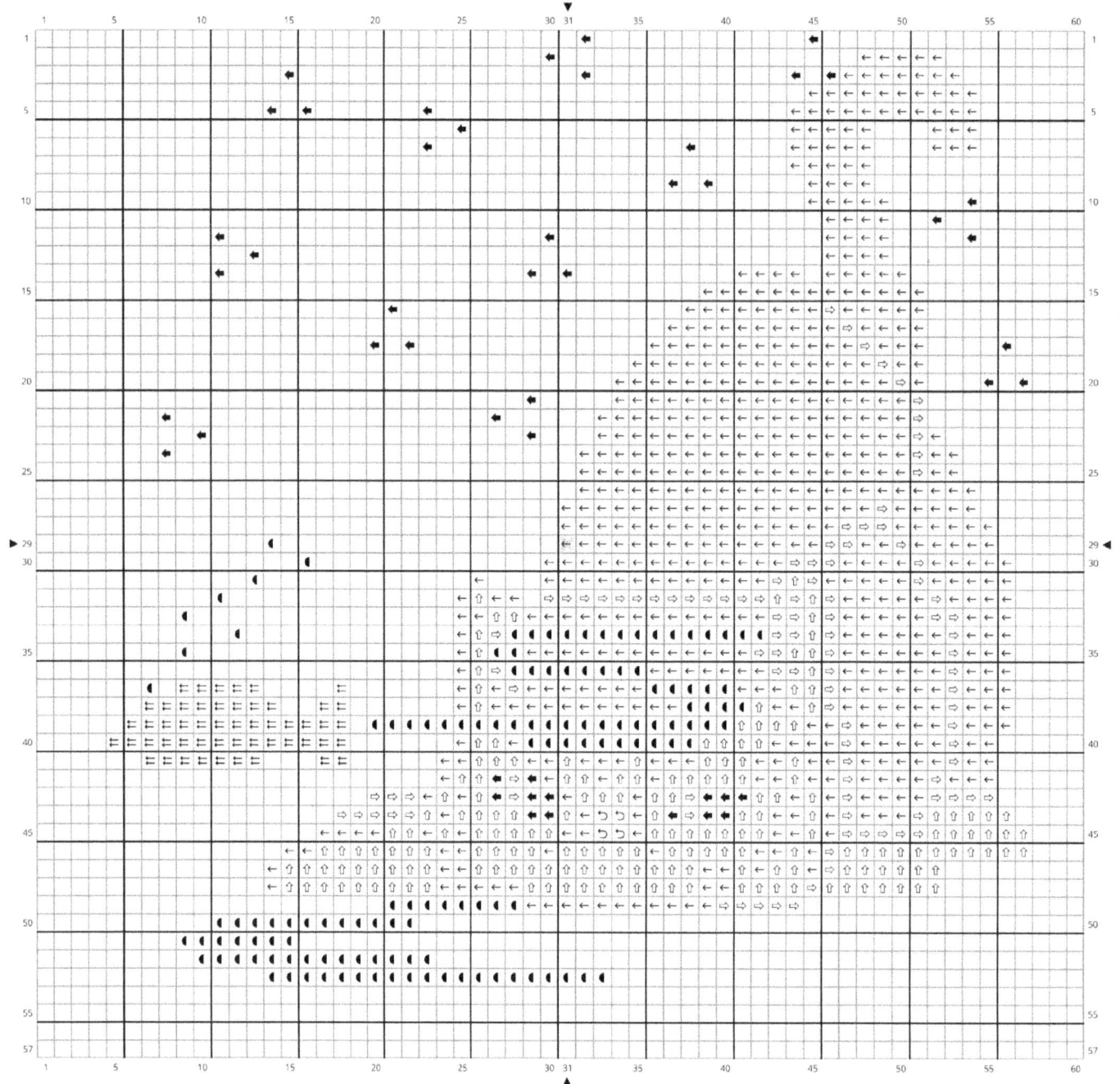

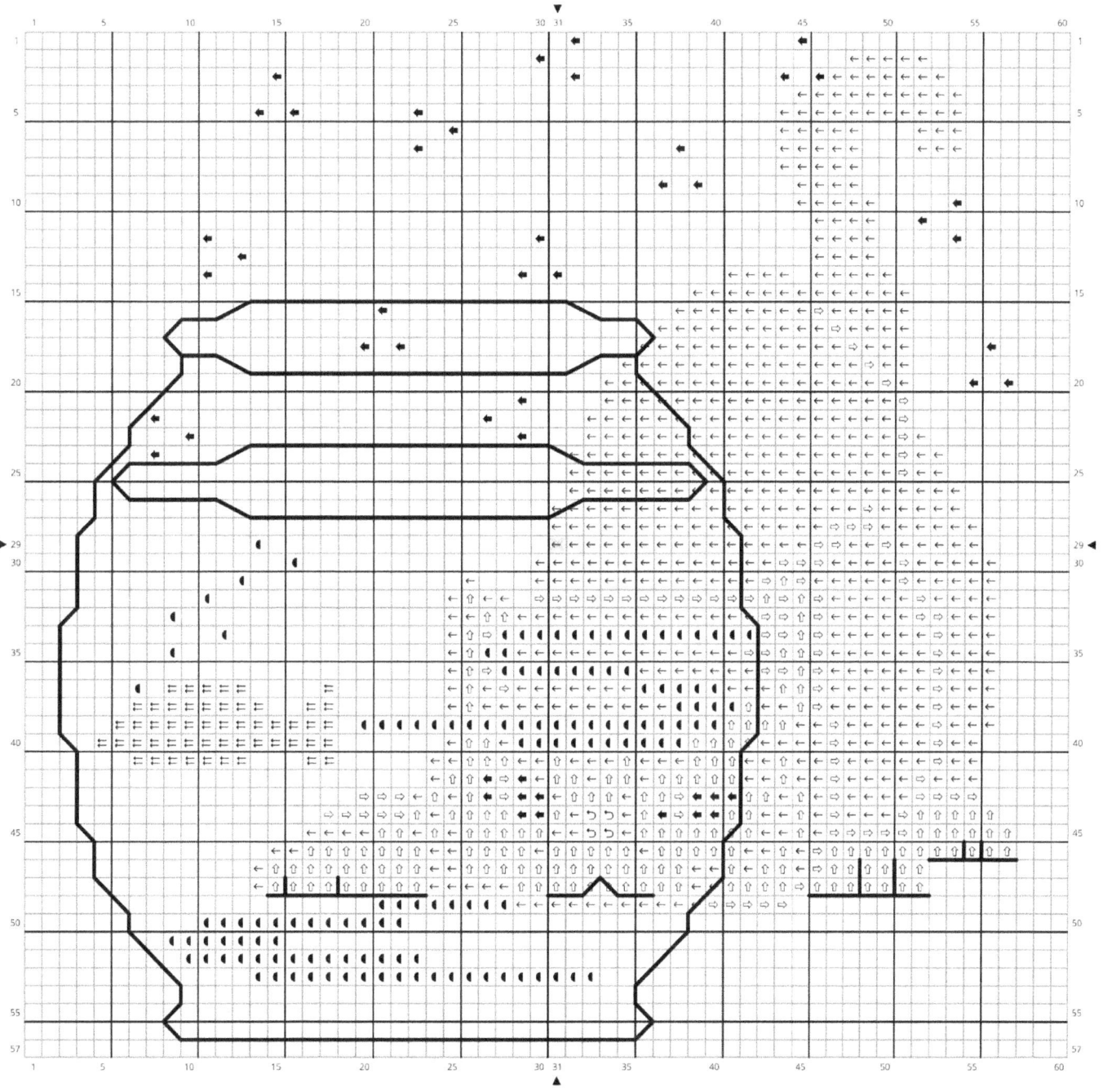

Curious Kitten

General Information

Fabric count: 14 count Aida

Stitches: 59 by 62

Total skeins: 9

Finished size: 4.2" by 4.4"

Total Stitches: 2,226

Floss type: DMC

DMC Embroidery Floss Color Code

⤿	D310	Black	Stitches: 10 – Skeins: 1
↗	D334	Baby Blue MD	Stitches: 10 – Skeins: 1
◉	D601	Cranberry DK	Stitches: 6 – Skeins: 1
⤴	D728	Topaz	Stitches: 265 – Skeins: 1
☐	D739	Tan UL VY LT	Stitches: 435 – Skeins: 1
↧	D898	Coffee Brown VY DK	Stitches: 34 – Skeins: 1
◣	D909	Emerald Green VY DK	Stitches: 258 – Skeins: 1
◀	D975	Golden Brown DK	Stitches: 535 – Skeins: 1
◆	D976	Golden Brown MD	Stitches: 673 – Skeins: 1

Back Stitching

Curious Kitten has no backstitching

Curious Kitten

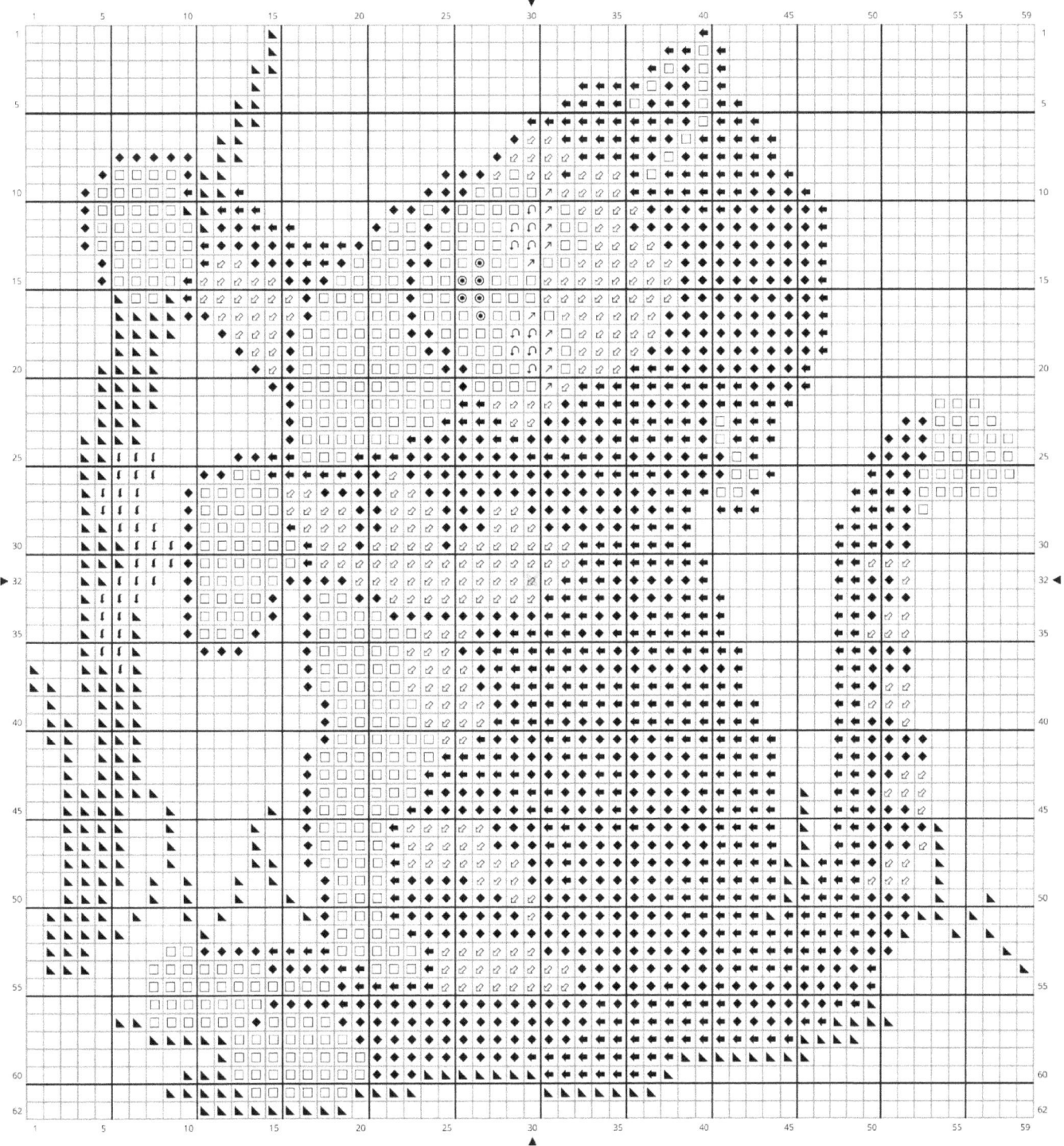